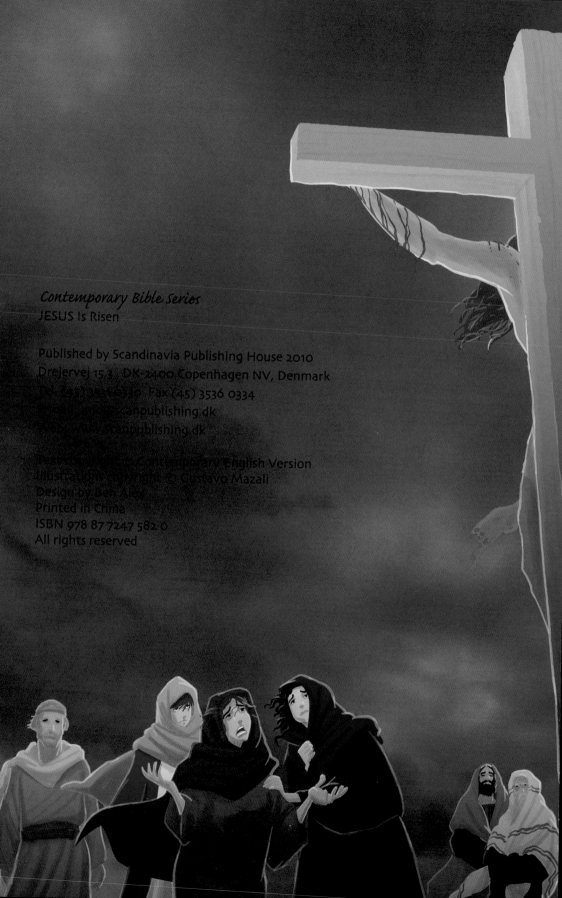

Contemporary Bible Series
JESUS Is Risen

Published by Scandinavia Publishing House 2010
Drejervej 15,3 DK-2400 Copenhagen NV, Denmark
Tel. (45) 3536 0340 Fax (45) 3536 0334
E-mail: info@scanpublishing.dk
Web: www.scanpublishing.dk

Text: Based on Contemporary English Version
Illustration Copyright © Gustavo Mazali
Design by Ben Alex
Printed in China
ISBN 978 87 7247 582 0

JESUS

Is Risen

Contemporary English Version

Contents

A Special Meal is Prepared

Luke 22:7-13

The day had come for the Passover. Jesus said to Peter and John, "Go and prepare the Passover meal for us to eat." They asked, "Where do you want us to prepare it?" Jesus told them, "As you go into the city, you will meet a man carrying a jar of water. Follow him into the house and say to the owner, 'Our teacher wants to know where he can eat the Passover meal with his disciples.' The owner will take you upstairs and show you a large room ready for you to use. Prepare the meal there." Peter and John left. They found everything just as Jesus had told them, and they prepared the Passover meal.

4

A New Command

John 13: 31-35

Jesus said, "Now the Son of Man will be given glory. Then after God is given glory because of him, God will bring glory to him. God will do it very soon. My children, I will be with you for a little while longer. Then you will look for me, but you won't find me. I tell you just as I told the people, 'You cannot go where I am going.' But I am giving you a new command. You must love each other just as I have loved you. If you love each other, everyone will know that you are my disciples."

The Leaders Shall Serve

Luke 22:14, 24-30

When the time came for Jesus and the apostles to eat, the apostles got into an argument about which one of them was the greatest. Jesus told them,

"Foreign kings order their people around. Powerful rulers call themselves everyone's friends. Don't be like them. The most important one of you should be like the least important. Your leader should be like a servant.

Who do people think is the greatest – a person who is served or one who serves? Isn't it the one who is served? But I have been with you as a servant. You have stayed with me in all my troubles. So I will give you the right to rule as kings, just as my Father has given me the right to rule as a king. You will eat and drink with me in my kingdom. And you will each sit on a throne to judge the twelve tribes of Israel."

Jesus Washes the Disciples' Feet

John 13:1-9

Jesus knew that the time had come for him to leave this world and to return to the Father. He had always loved his followers in this world and he loved them to the very end. The evening meal was being served, and the devil had already made Judas betray Jesus. Jesus knew that God had given him complete power and that he had come from God and was going back to God.

So Jesus got up, removed his outer garment, and wrapped a towel around his waist. He put some water into a large bowl. Then he began washing his disciples' feet and drying them with the towel he was wearing. Simon Peter asked, "Lord, are you going to wash my feet?" Jesus answered, "You don't really know what I am doing, but later you will understand."

"You will never wash my feet!" Peter replied.

"If I don't wash you," Jesus told him, "you don't really belong to me."

Peter said, "Lord, then don't just wash my feet. Wash my hands and my head."

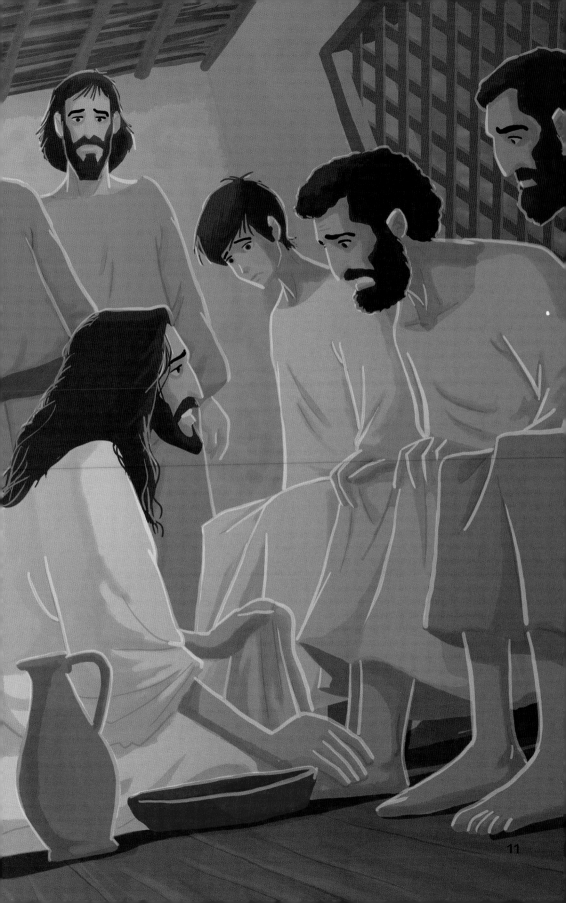

Jesus Sets the Example

John 13:12-17

After Jesus had washed his disciples' feet and had put his outer garment back on, he sat down again. Then he said, "Do you understand what I have done? You call me your teacher and Lord, and you should. That is who I am. If your Lord and teacher has washed your feet, do the same for each other. I have set the example. You should do for each other exactly what I have done for you. "I tell you for certain that servants are not greater than their master. Messengers are not greater than the one who sent them. You know these things. God will bless you if you do them."

The Lord's Supper

Mark 14:18-25

While Jesus and the twelve disciples were eating together that evening, Jeseus said, "The one who will betray me is now eating with me." This made the disciples sad. They each said to Jesus, "You surely don't mean me!" He answered, "It is one of you twelve men who is eating from this dish with me. The Son of Man will die, just as the Scriptures say. But it is going to be terrible for the one who betrays me. That man would be better off if he had never been born."

During the meal Jesus took some bread in his hands. He blessed the bread and broke it. Then he gave it to his disciples and said, "Take this. It is my body." Jesus picked up a cup of wine and gave thanks to God. He gave it to his disciples. They all drank some. Then he said, "This is my blood, which is poured out for many people. With it God makes his promise. From now on I will not drink any wine until I drink new wine in God's kingdom."

Peter Will Deny Jesus

Mark 14:26-31

The disciples sang a hymn and went out to the Mount of Olives. Jesus said to his disciples, "All of you will reject me, as the Scriptures say, 'I will strike down the shepherd, and the sheep will be scattered.' But after I am raised to life, I will go ahead of you to Galilee."

Peter spoke up, "Even if all the others reject you, I never will!"

Jesus replied, "This very night before a rooster crows twice, you will say three times that

you don't know me." Peter was so sure of himself that he said, "Even if I have to die with you, I will never say that I don't know you!" All the other disciples said the same thing.

A Home in Heaven

John 14:1-6

Jesus said to his disciples, "Don't be worried! Have faith in God and have faith in me. There are many rooms in my Father's house. I wouldn't tell you this, unless it was true. I am going there to prepare a place for each of you. After I have done this, I will come back and take you with me. Then we will be together. You know the way to where I am going."

Thomas said, "Lord, we don't even know where you are going! How can we know the way?"

"I am the way, the truth, and the life!" Jesus answered. "Without me, no one can go to the Father."

Jesus Prays for His Followers

John 17:1-18:1

After Jesus had finished speaking to his disciples, he looked up toward heaven and prayed, "Father, the time has come for you to bring glory to your Son, in order that he may bring glory to you. And you gave him power over all people so that he would give eternal life to everyone you give him. Eternal life is to know you, the only true God, and to know Jesus Christ, the one you sent.

"You have given me some followers from this world, and I have shown them what you are like. They were yours, but you gave them to me, and they have obeyed you. They know that I came from you, and they believe that you are the one who sent me. Holy Father, I am coming to you. But my followers are still in the world. So keep them safe by the power of the name that you have given me. I also pray for those who will have faith because of what my followers say about me that they will be one with each other, just as you and I are one. Your word is the truth. So let this truth make them completely yours."

When Jesus had finished praying, he and his disciples crossed the Kidron Valley and went into a garden.

21

The Disciples Fall Asleep

Mark 14:33-42

Jesus took along Peter, James, and John. Jesus was troubled and told them, "I am so sad that I feel as if I am dying. Stay here and keep awake with me." Jesus walked on a little way. Then he knelt down on the ground and prayed, "Father, if it is possible, don't let this happen to me. Don't make me suffer by having me drink from this cup. But do what you want, and not what I want."

When Jesus came back, he found the disciples sleeping. He said to Simon Peter, "Are you asleep? Can't you stay awake for just one hour? Stay awake and pray that you won't be tested. You want to do what is right, but you are weak." Jesus went back and prayed the same prayer. But when he returned to the disciples, he found them sleeping again. When Jesus returned to the disciples the third time, he said, "The time has come for the Son of Man to be handed over to sinners. Get up! Let's go. The one who will betray me is already here."

Betrayed With a Kiss

John 18:2-8; Matthew 26:48-49

Jesus often met in the garden with his disciples. Judas had promised to betray Jesus. So he went to the garden with some Roman soldiers and temple

24

police, who had been sent by the chief priests and the Pharisees. They carried torches, lanterns, and weapons. Judas had told the soldiers ahead of time, "Arrest the man I greet with a kiss."

Jesus already knew everything that was going to happen. He asked, "Who are you looking for?" They answered, "We are looking for Jesus from Nazareth!"

Jesus told them, "I am Jesus!"

At once they all backed away and fell to the ground.

Jesus again asked, "Who are you looking for?"

"We are looking for Jesus from Nazareth," they answered.

This time Jesus replied, "I have already told you that I am Jesus. If I am the one you are looking for, let these others go." Judas walked right up to Jesus and said, "Hello, teacher." Then Judas kissed him.

Jesus is Taken Away

John 18:10-11; Luke 22:51-53

Simon Peter had brought along a sword. He pulled it out and struck at the servant of the high priest. The servant's name was Malchus. Peter cut off his right ear. Jesus told Peter, "Put your sword away. I must drink from the cup that the Father has given me." Then he touched the servant's ear and healed it.

Jesus spoke to the chief priests, the temple police, and the leaders who had come to arrest him. He said, "Why do you come out with swords and clubs and treat me like a criminal? I was with you every day in the temple, and you didn't arrest me. But this is your time, and darkness is in control."

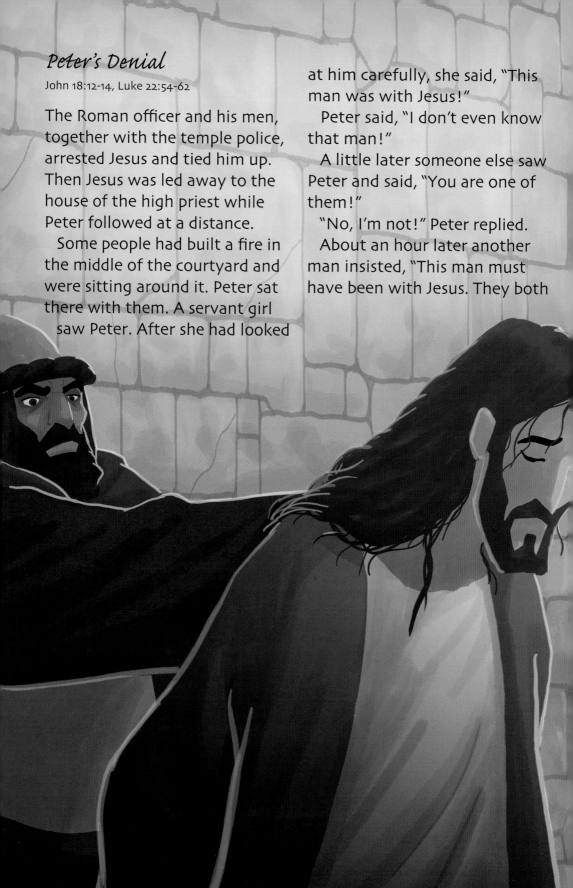

Peter's Denial
John 18:12-14, Luke 22:54-62

The Roman officer and his men, together with the temple police, arrested Jesus and tied him up. Then Jesus was led away to the house of the high priest while Peter followed at a distance.

Some people had built a fire in the middle of the courtyard and were sitting around it. Peter sat there with them. A servant girl saw Peter. After she had looked at him carefully, she said, "This man was with Jesus!"

Peter said, "I don't even know that man!"

A little later someone else saw Peter and said, "You are one of them!"

"No, I'm not!" Peter replied.

About an hour later another man insisted, "This man must have been with Jesus. They both

come from Galilee."
   Peter replied, "I don't know what you are talking about!"
   Right then a rooster crowed. Peter remembered that the Lord had said, "Before a rooster crows tomorrow morning, you will say three times that you don't know me." Peter went out and cried.

Jesus is Questioned

Mark 14:53-65, 15:1

The chief priests, the nation's leaders, and the teachers of the Law of Moses all met together. They tried to find someone to accuse Jesus of a crime so they could put him to death. Finally some men stood up and lied about him.

They said, "We heard him say he would tear down this temple that we built. He also claimed that in three days he would build another one without any help." The high priest stood up in the council and asked Jesus, "Why don't you say something in your own defense? Don't you hear the charges they are making against you?"

Jesus kept quiet and did not say a word.

The high priest asked him another question, "Are you the Messiah, the Son of the glorious God?"

"Yes, I am!" Jesus answered, "Soon you will see the Son of Man sitting at the right side of God All-Powerful and coming with the clouds of heaven."

At once the high priest ripped his robe apart and shouted, "Why do we need more witnesses? You heard him claim to be God! What is your decision?"

They all agreed that he should be put to death. Some of the people started spitting on Jesus. They blindfolded him. They hit him with their fists. Then the guards took Jesus and beat him. They tied Jesus up and led him off to Pilate.

31

Jesus is Sent to Herod

Luke 23:7-12

Pilate learned that Jesus came from the region ruled by Herod. So he sent Jesus to Herod in Jerusalem. Herod had wanted to see Jesus and was very happy because he finally had this chance. He had heard many things about Jesus and hoped to see him work a miracle. Herod asked him a lot of questions, but Jesus did not answer.

Then the chief priests and the teachers of the Law of Moses stood up and accused him of all kinds of bad things. Herod and his soldiers made fun of Jesus and insulted him. They put a fine robe on him and sent him back to Pilate. That same day Herod and Pilate became friends even though they had been enemies before this.

Pilate Tries to Free Jesus

John 18:28-40

It was early in the morning when Jesus was taken to the building where the Roman governor stayed. The crowd waited outside. Pilate came out and asked, "What charges are you bringing against this man?"

They answered, "He is a criminal! That's why we brought him to you."

Pilate told them, "Take him and judge him by your own laws."

The crowd replied, "We are not allowed to put anyone to death." Pilate then went back inside. He called Jesus over and asked, "Are you the king of the Jews?"

Jesus answered, "Are you asking this on your own or did someone tell you about me?"

"You know I'm not a Jew!" Pilate said. "Your own people and the chief priests brought you to me. What have you done?"

Jesus answered, "My kingdom doesn't belong to this world. If it did, my followers would have fought to keep me from being handed over to the Jewish leaders. No, my kingdom doesn't belong to this world."

"So you are a king," Pilate replied.

"You are saying that I am a king," Jesus told him. "I was born into this world to tell about the truth. And everyone who belongs to the truth knows my voice."

Pilate went back out and said, "I don't find

this man guilty of anything! And since I usually set a prisoner free for you at Passover, would you like for me to set free the king of the Jews?" They shouted, "No, not him! We want Barabbas." Barabbas was a terrorist.

Jesus is Sentenced to Death

John 19:1-16

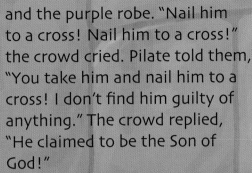

Pilate gave orders for Jesus to be beaten with a whip. The soldiers made a crown out of thorn branches and put it on Jesus. Then they put a purple robe on him. Once again Pilate went out to the crowd. He said, "I will have Jesus brought out to you again. Then you can see for yourselves that I have not found him guilty." Jesus came out wearing the crown of thorns and the purple robe. "Nail him to a cross! Nail him to a cross!" the crowd cried. Pilate told them, "You take him and nail him to a cross! I don't find him guilty of anything." The crowd replied, "He claimed to be the Son of God!"

When Pilate heard this he was terrified. He went back inside and asked Jesus, "Where are you from?" Jesus did not answer.

"Why won't you answer my question?" Pilate asked. "Don't you know that I have the power to let you go free or to nail you to a cross?"

Jesus replied, "If God had not given you the power, you couldn't do anything at all to me. But the one who handed me over to you did something even worse."

Pilate wanted to set Jesus free. But the crowd again yelled, "If you set this man free, you are no friend of the Emperor! Anyone who claims to be a king is an enemy of the Emperor. Kill him! Kill him!"

"So you want me to nail your king to a cross?" Pilate asked. The chief priests replied, "The Emperor is our king!" Then Pilate handed Jesus over to be nailed to a cross.

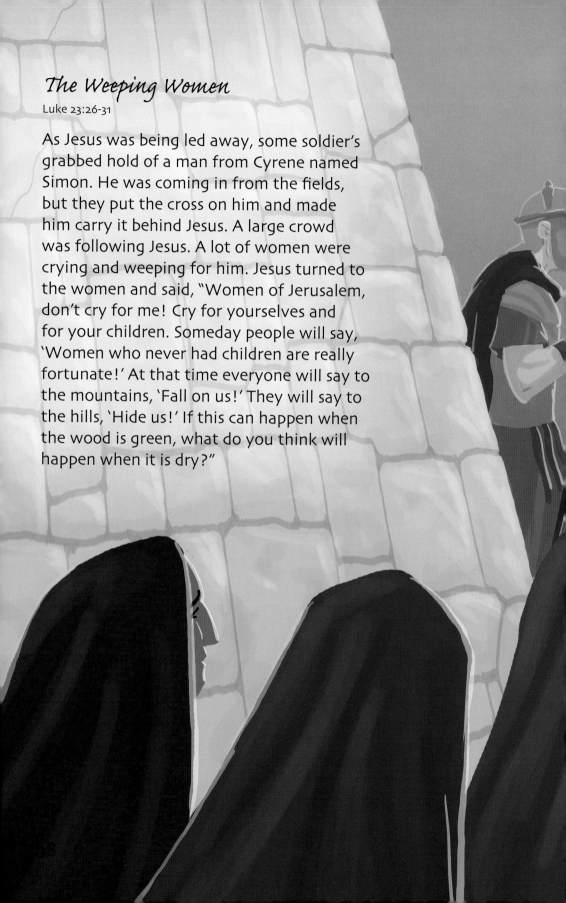

The Weeping Women
Luke 23:26-31

As Jesus was being led away, some soldier's grabbed hold of a man from Cyrene named Simon. He was coming in from the fields, but they put the cross on him and made him carry it behind Jesus. A large crowd was following Jesus. A lot of women were crying and weeping for him. Jesus turned to the women and said, "Women of Jerusalem, don't cry for me! Cry for yourselves and for your children. Someday people will say, 'Women who never had children are really fortunate!' At that time everyone will say to the mountains, 'Fall on us!' They will say to the hills, 'Hide us!' If this can happen when the wood is green, what do you think will happen when it is dry?"

39

Jesus is Nailed to a Cross

Luke 23:32-38

Two criminals were led out to be put to death with Jesus. The soldiers came to the place called "The Skull." There they nailed Jesus to a cross. They also nailed the two criminals to crosses, one on each side of Jesus.

Jesus said, "Father, forgive these people! They don't know what they're doing."

While the crowd stood there watching Jesus, the soldiers gambled for his clothes. The leaders insulted him by saying, "He saved others. Now he should save himself, if he really is God's chosen Messiah!" The soldiers made fun of Jesus. They said, "If you are the king of the Jews, save yourself!" Above him was a sign that said: This Is the King of the Jews.

Jesus Dies

Luke 23:39-44; John 19:28-30

One of the criminals hanging there also insulted Jesus by saying, "Aren't you the Messiah? Save yourself and save us!" But the other criminal told the first one, "Don't you fear God? Aren't you getting the same punishment as this man? We got what was coming to us, but he didn't do anything wrong." Then he said to Jesus, "Remember me when you come into power!" Jesus replied, "I promise that today you will be with me in paradise."

Around noon the sky turned dark and stayed that way until the middle of the afternoon. Jesus knew that he had now finished his work. In order to make the Scriptures come true, he said, "I am thirsty!" Someone soaked a sponge in a jar of wine and held it up to Jesus' mouth on the stem of a hyssop plant. After Jesus drank the wine, he said, "Everything is done!" He bowed his head and died.

The Earth Trembles

Matthew 27:51-54

The moment Jesus died, the curtain in the temple was torn in two from top to bottom. The earth shook, and rocks split apart. Graves opened, and many of God's people were raised to life. Then after Jesus had risen to life, they came out of their graves and went into the holy city, where they were seen by many people. The officer and the soldiers guarding Jesus felt the earthquake and saw everything else that happened. They were frightened and said, "This man really was God's Son!"

44

45

Jesus is Buried

John 19:31-34; Matthew 27:57-61

The next day would be both a Sabbath and the Passover. It was a special day for the Jewish people, and they did not want the bodies to stay on the crosses during that day. They asked Pilate to break the men's legs and take their bodies down. The soldiers first broke the legs of the other two men who were nailed there. But when they came to Jesus, they saw that he was already dead, and they did not break his legs.

That evening a rich disciple named Joseph from the town of Arimathea went and asked for Jesus' body. Pilate gave orders for it to be given to Joseph. Joseph took the body and wrapped it in a clean linen cloth. Then he put the body in his own tomb that had been cut into solid rock and had never been used. He rolled a big stone against the entrance to the tomb and went away.

47

Jesus Has Risen

Matthew 28:1-10

It was almost daybreak on Sunday when Mary Magdalene and the other Mary went to see the tomb. Suddenly a strong earthquake struck. The Lord's angel came down from heaven. He rolled away the stone and sat on it. The angel looked as bright as lightning. His clothes were white as snow. The guards shook from fear and fell down as though they were dead.

The angel said to the women, "Don't be afraid! I know you are looking for Jesus, who was nailed to a cross. He isn't here! God has raised him to life, just as Jesus said he would. Come; see the place where his body was lying. Now hurry! Tell his disciples that he has been raised to life and is on his way to Galilee. Go there, and you will see him. That is what I came to tell you."

The women were frightened and yet very happy. They hurried from the tomb and ran to tell Jesus' disciples. Suddenly Jesus met them and greeted them. They held on to his feet and worshiped him. Then Jesus said, "Don't be afraid! Tell my followers to go to Galilee. They will see me there."

48

49

The Empty Tomb

John 20:2-18

Mary Magdalene ran to Simon Peter and to Jesus' favorite disciple and said, "They have taken the Lord from the tomb!" Peter and the other disciple started for the tomb. The other disciple got there first. He bent over and saw the strips of linen cloth lying inside the tomb, but he did not go in.

When Simon Peter got there, he went into the tomb and saw the strips of cloth. He also saw the piece of cloth that had been used to cover Jesus' face. It was rolled up and in a place by itself. The disciple who got there first then went into the tomb, and when he saw it, he believed. At that time Peter and the other disciple did not know that the Scriptures said Jesus would rise to life. The two of them went back to the other disciples.

Jesus Appears
to the Disciples

John 20:19; Luke 24:37-45; John 20:21-23

The disciples were afraid of the
Jewish leaders. On the evening
of that same Sunday they locked
themselves in a room. Suddenly,
Jesus appeared in the middle of
the group. They were terrified
because they thought they were
seeing a ghost.

Jesus said, "Why are you so
frightened? Why do you doubt?
Look at my hands and my feet
and see who I am! Touch me and
find out for yourselves. Ghosts
don't have flesh and bones as
you see I have."

After Jesus said this, he showed

them his hands and his feet. The disciples were so amazed that they could not believe it. Then Jesus asked them, "Do you have something to eat?" They gave him a piece of baked fish. He took it and ate it as they watched. He said, "I am sending you, just as the Father has sent me."

Then he breathed on the disciples and said, "Receive the Holy Spirit. If you forgive anyone's sins, they will be forgiven. But if you don't forgive their sins, they will not be forgiven."

Thomas Touches Jesus' Wounds

John 20:24-29

Although Thomas was one of the twelve disciples, he wasn't with the others when Jesus appeared to them. So they told him, "We have seen the Lord!"

But Thomas said, "First I must see the nail scars in his hands and touch them with my finger. I must put my hand where the spear went into his side. I won't believe unless I do this!"

A week later the disciples were together again. This time Thomas was with them. Jesus

came in while the doors were still locked and stood in the middle of the group. He greeted his disciples and said to Thomas, "Put your finger here and look at my hands! Put your hand into my side. Stop doubting and have faith!" Thomas replied, "You are my Lord and my God!" Jesus said, "Thomas, do you have faith because you have seen me? The people who have faith in me without seeing me are the ones who are really blessed!"

A Net Full of Fish

John 21:1-14

Jesus appeared to his disciples later along the shore of Lake Tiberias. Simon Peter said, "I'm going fishing!" The others said, "We will go with you." They went out in their boat. But they didn't catch a thing that night.

Early the next morning Jesus stood on the shore. The disciples did not realize who he was. Jesus shouted, "Friends, have you caught anything?"

"No!" they answered. He told them, "Let your net down on the right side of your boat and you will catch some fish." They did. The net was so full of fish that they could not drag it up into the boat. Jesus' favorite disciple told Peter, "It's the Lord!" When Simon heard that it was the Lord, he jumped into the water. The other disciples stayed in the boat and dragged in the net full of fish. In it there were one hundred fifty-three large fish, but still the net did not rip.

When the disciples got out of the boat, they saw some bread and a charcoal fire with fish on it. Jesus told his disciples "Bring some of the fish you just caught. Come and eat!" None of the disciples dared ask who he was. They knew he was the Lord. Jesus took the bread in his hands and gave some of it to his disciples. He did the same with the fish. This was the third time that Jesus appeared to his disciples after he was raised from death.

Jesus and Peter

John 21:15-19

When Jesus and his disciples had finished eating, he asked, "Simon, do you love me more than the others do?" Simon Peter answered, "Yes, Lord, you know I do!"

"Then feed my lambs," Jesus said.

Jesus asked a second time, "Simon son of John, do you love me?" Peter answered, "Yes, Lord, you know I love you!"

"Then take care of my sheep," Jesus told him.

Jesus asked a third time, "Simon son of John, do you love me?"

Peter was hurt because Jesus had asked him three times if

he loved him. So he told Jesus, "Lord, you know everything. You know I love you."

Jesus replied, "Feed my sheep. I tell you for certain that when you were a young man, you dressed yourself and went wherever you wanted to go. But when you are old, you will hold out your hands. Then others will wrap your belt around you and lead you where you don't want to go."

Jesus said this to tell how Peter would die and bring honor to God.

Jesus Returns to God

Acts 1:3-11

For forty days after Jesus had suffered and died, he proved in many ways that he had been raised from death. He appeared to his apostles and spoke to them about God's kingdom.

While he was still with them, he said, "Don't leave Jerusalem yet. Wait here for the Father to give you the Holy Spirit, just as I told you he has promised to do. John baptized with water, but in a few days you will be baptized with the Holy Spirit."

The apostles asked Jesus, "Lord, are you going to give Israel its own king again?"

Jesus said to them, "You don't need to know the time of those events that only the Father controls. But the Holy Spirit will come upon you and give you power. Then you will tell everyone about me in Jerusalem, in all Judea, in Samaria, and everywhere in the world."

After Jesus had said this, he was taken up into a cloud. They could not see him, but the disciples kept looking up into the sky. Suddenly two men dressed in white clothes were standing beside them. They said, "Why are you men from Galilee standing here and looking up into the sky? Jesus has been taken to heaven. But he will come back in the same way that you have seen him go."

The Contemporary Bible Series